Sad Asian Music

poems by

Steve Fujimura

Finishing Line Press
Georgetown, Kentucky

Sad Asian Music

ACKNOWLEDGMENTS

Some poems in this book originally appeared in the following publications:

New American Writing: "An Autobiographical Conversation"

Milvia Street Art & Literary Journal: "Wayne"

Written Here: The Community of Writers Poetry Review: "Shame"

Essential Truths: The Bay Area in Color: "Fred Korematsu Day, Jan 30"

Publisher: Leah Huete de Maines
Editor: Christen Kincaid
Cover Art: Hideo Kobashigawa, *Childhood Memory: 3 or 4 Years old
at Arizona*
Author Photo: Amanda Mei Kim
Cover Design: Elizabeth Maines McCleavy

Order online: www.finishinglinepress.com
also available on amazon.com

Author inquiries and mail orders:
Finishing Line Press
P. O. Box 1626
Georgetown, Kentucky 40324
U. S. A.

Table of Contents

For my mother

Sayeko Katashima

who renamed herself:

Tara Fujimura

(1944-2019)

Japanese American

Japanese American tongue

Japanese American freedom

Japanese American verse

Japanese American dream

Japanese American time

Japanese American way

Japanese American hair

Japanese American song

Japanese American writer

Japanese American love

Japanese American beauty

Japanese American baggage

Japanese American rainbow

Japanese American movement

Japanese American laughter

Japanese American heart

Japanese American belief

Japanese American remake

Japanese American skin

Japanese American awesome

Japanese American suicide

Japanese American light

Japanese American cream

Japanese American menu

Japanese American double

Japanese American thought

Japanese American sex

Japanese American scenery

Japanese American stability

Japanese American epic

Japanese American dinner

Japanese American memory

Japanese American pillow

Japanese American chocolate

Japanese American burden

Japanese American make-up

Japanese American umph

Japanese American future

Japanese American wannabe

Japanese American scandal

Japanese American sweetheart

Japanese American original

Japanese American morsel

Japanese American drive-in

Japanese American riot

Japanese American enough

Will $20K—make
you forget it—keep
you quiet in the office—
write your perfect poem—

17 Reasons Why Iris Chang Still Appears

for Iris Chang and Wing-Tek Lum

I read her book *The Rape of Nanking.*

I believe she did not commit suicide as reported.

I remember her fear-glazed eyes when I saw her in the bookstore promoting her last book *The Chinese in America.*

I felt perceived as guilty for being Japanese when I walked past the event space where she was speaking.

I read in a biography by her mother that on that final book tour Iris encountered a threatening man who said "You should join us (if you know what's good for you)," and Iris, stunned, walked away.

I have read a series of brutal and graphic poems by Wing-Tek Lum who has spent 10 years writing about the Nanjing massacre after he read *The Rape of Nanking.*

I think of her ghost while driving on Highway 17 near where her body shot through the mouth was found.

I apologize for that last image (modeled after Wing-Tek Lum's), but should you accept this apology?

I remember a coworker stating that Iris took her own life because of the things she wrote about, and I thought that was what we were supposed to think.

I have read that Japanese officials continue to deny the Nanjing massacre today, or downplay it, and that old right-wing factions may try to silence you if you say otherwise.

I wonder if we must be prepared to give up our lives in mass protest when those in power finally achieve what they have been threatening all along.

I attended an international conference on "Asian American Studies in Asia" in Taipei, where two Taiwanese participants said they could never go to Japan because of what the government there had done to Taiwanese and Chinese people in the last century.

I met a filmmaker from Indonesia who jokingly stated that the Japanese were the "Nazis of Asia."

I once drunkenly proclaimed my strange feelings of guilt about being Japanese and about Japan's historical atrocities while eating at a German restaurant in San Jose.

I am not from Japan—although I have affinities, and my relationship to the internment is a psychic split between us—the J and the JA.

I no longer believe in coincidence so when I thought about Iris recently while driving on Highway 17, a route I take weekly, it was part intention, part providence.

I will likely write about this in whatever form it takes, with as many forms as it takes.

truth: belief
    crime: teeth

Occupy News Fall

At the Port of Oakland—four people—in one of several Occupy buses—blocking the unloading of shipments—according to Scott—had an argument about—tactics. This occurred when the Teamsters—in large empty trucks broke—up the group—of buses—by speeding—past them—aggressively. Dispatchers—told the Greyhound drivers—not to let Occupiers—off and to leave—the Port—altogether. One Occupier—riding the bus—singing—was an elderly Mexican American woman who was asked by—an agitated—white woman—to stop. The white woman—in turn was reprimanded—by a middle-aged, white man—to let the older—woman sing. The white man was told—by an African-American—butch lesbian—to shut his mouth—Scott said. Occupiers—have been warned by group leaders when arrests are imminent—and people of color are encouraged to leave—en-masse before—police arrive. The difference in treatment that non-white people receive—when arrested—by authorities is recognized—as a threat to the—Occupy movement—David Solnit—Occupy trainer—acknowledged—said Scott.

A Berkeley poet—whose poet partner was pushed to the ground—was jabbed just hard enough in the ribs—by predominantly—white men and a single woman of color—in Darth—Vader—riot—gear—he wrote. The force—by which the Alameda sheriffs pushed back—with batons—an unarmed populace of students—in their indiscriminate beating of—men and women—shocked the—former—Poet Laureate. Another poet—a woman—was dragged by the hair—by sheriffs—when she offered herself up—for arrest. A fourth poet—got a rib—broken—whether by police or—by other means—is not clear. The—Poet Laureate—said that—the entire California university system—is paralyzed by—a minority of legislators—whose only idea—is that they don't want to pay—one more cent—in taxes.

A young woman—danced in the middle of Market St. as Occupy—protestors shut down traffic—to celebrate the—one-year—anniversary—of the Occupy movement—Monday, September 17, 2012. Standing—with—Others—another commemorator—held a sign—HELLS FARGO—in front of the bank—patrolled by a phalanx of—helmeted—police. Outraged seniors—experiencing real estate foreclosure—joined the protest—on Van Ness Ave. Another person in a black jacket—which on the back—read—PATIENTS—NOT—PROFITS—held an impromptu conference—in the financial—district.

Today—Sunday—on my way to lunch—a break from work—10 Occupiers sat peacefully—in front of the Post Office—in downtown—Santa Cruz. There were no signs—no police—only Occupiers saying hello—to passersby. One man—I see in the bookstore each week—and at city meetings on community TV. Middle-aged, he wears a Hawaiian shirt—and shorts—and often marches with young people for various causes. He stands out by his height—6+ feet—and blonde, pageboy haircut. I wonder if he needs to work for a living. I wonder where the other Occupiers—are?

1st stanza told by Occupier friend to author.
2nd stanza from "Poet-Bashing Police"—by Robert Hass—https://www.nytimes.com/2011/11/20/opinion/sunday/at-occupy-berkeley-beat-poets-has-new-meaning.html?pagewanted=all
3rd stanza from "Occupy San Francisco"—SFGate—Sept. 17, 2012
http://www.sfgate.com/bayarea/slideshow/Occupy-San-Francisco-49217.php#photo-3470276
4th stanza witnessed and interpreted by author in Santa Cruz, CA.

Fred Korematsu Day, Jan 30

it's JA day
every day, no, well
for those
with this skin
these names
and this history

and if yours
aren't with you
every day, then
what is
with you

Wayne

He died
young—24—due to
a civil war in the streets
between Black and white and
a few Koreans with guns on
LA rooftops and others
watched or ran and he
watched, ran, got a gun, too
against those who
beat Rodney King that night
beat him and went free
causing the riot
a white truck driver pulled
from his cab and stoned
and punched and kicked on TV
he watched that passively
as one could watch that
and it was painful
to the other him watching,
triggering a memory
he remembered a gun
dormant under a bed
a gun used for hunting
said the TV news
a gun that fired semi-automatic rounds
under and over police cars
injuring two officers at an armory
where he stopped to end
the force
of the state
he was in. We
figured it must make sense
at his age—24—depressed
a time that has been repeated again
and again
if only that were the sound of him
coming back again

from the fields where we played
among the strawberries

Mother Memory

my mother may be having
memory problems; is it
due to a lack of social contact,
yet she does have friends,
Mari, Kazuko, and another
whose name I forget—
our memory of a feeling without words
inspires loss, sadness?—
an only son and single mother—

meeting my father's mother for
the first time in 2009, she
remembers more than most
at her age, 96, we are lucky,
she tells her story, I record it
on video, a vulnerable medium
for memory

are we making new memories—
my mother and I?—
she seems to be going along
without attachment —
she tells me to stay at my new job
for the pension, she tells me not
to spend too much,
she reiterates not to waste
as if I had not heard her before, yet
she did call to make sure I returned
from my week-long trip okay,
she is not reading books anymore
after a lifetime of reading
she is soft-spoken, she still laughs
at my sarcasm

my partner and I watch the newest *Jane Eyre* movie
and I remember how my mother
used to watch different versions of this film

how much I believe my mother
identified with Jane who ran away from Rochester
and briefly lived in a modest space alone
which my mother sort of lives in now
in a small apartment among other seniors
no need for men, she intimates,
except for me who takes her out to lunch or dinner sometimes
I think my mother used to identify with Mary Tyler Moore in
        the 1970s
and with Audrey Hepburn in *Breakfast at Tiffany's*
I'm sure the internment plays a part
today I no longer know

if my mother is losing her memory, then perhaps those older
memories remain intact, not the newer ones
our more recent outings together
she may have forgotten, perhaps
even her visit to Taiwan seeing us
during Chinese New Year
I am reluctant to confirm this with her—

is that how memory fades

mention the
    fading trees

Zen Stereotype #7

For eternal truth—
Oh, the morning
—*Mandala*, dir. Im Kwon-Taek—

"What's happening, Hot Stuff?"
—Gedde Watanabe, *Sixteen Candles*—

you were let go from your job
by hipster managers
not the "best fit"
you were told
that's it
and what if you were the sole male of color
what part was due to race, and what was due
to performance, or was your performance
your race

was your Asian face too much for them
your voice too fluent, too rich beyond
the pale of Hollywood
or were you not Asian enough
not Murakami enough or
worse (not) like Long-Duk Dong
(at the event
for her husband's book
you saw Molly Ringwald
and you wanted to ask her
how's Gedde?)
did they care to know the difference between
you and the Japanese lamps
that one of them bought
for his hipster living room
when one of them asked out loud
"is 'chink in the armor' racist?"
and another answered "no!"
you said
"it depends on the context"

and another noted a website
of 100 racist sayings
as anthropologically cool
that's the kind of fucked-up, asinine daily
conversation you had to endure
do you judge them too cruelly
this group of people who
believe they're all so prized
who would choose their society
by mouse clicks
in 2013, in this increasingly
bullshit city fog

Ah, for eternal truth
Oh, the morning

Oh Battlestar Galactica

Edward James Olmos
the only man of color not relegated to playing a Cylon
or an extra in the crowd. Of them, a handful of Asian men
without mouths apparently, yet eyes, looking upon
Starbuck, Lee, Sharon and others
wondering when to tell them his true feelings
for them. You might ask, "Is he even human?"
The Asian man walking to a computer terminal on deck
behind the XO, a Cylon in secret, or maybe
that was the Asian man carrying a wrench
to fix the FTL drive. How did George Takei
have it so good 40 years ago as Mr. Sulu, even
commanded his own ship in the Star Trek franchise?

Grace Park (Korean American Canadian) and Rekha Sharma (South
        Asian Canadian)
play Cylons, one who is half trusted by the humans, and
the other who is entirely incognito among them. They are paired in love
with white men among the predominantly white humans
who represent surviving humanity. That the rest of surviving humanity
resembles the rest of the United States (mainly white) is a miscalculation
at worst, an irony at best? Yet Sharon (Grace Park) is replicated many
times as Boomer and Cylon Eight, the actress multiplied into many copies
by special effects, as an Asian horde might appear. And Rekha Sharma is
duplicitous even murderous and longs for love as Cylon Tory. Together
they provide gender/color diversity in a show described as socially
progressive yet they fulfill deep-seated, white-programmed stereotypes
about race in America. Why couldn't Grace and Rekha be human rather
than Cylon Others? Why couldn't they find love among human & Cylon
men of color? And where do the Asian men stand as quiet eyes gazing
upon their destiny controlled by humans and Cylons alike? You might
say the show is a metaphor, casting is superfluous. But would you watch
a program in which the rest of surviving humanity were predominantly
Asian with scant whites? I would, because that reflects the globe, earth,
toward which our protagonists strive as the humans=whites, run from the
Cylons=people of color, as from city to suburb, or in this case Caprica to
Earth.

Rick Worthy (African American)
plays Simon, Cylon Four, a medical doctor who removes Starbuck's
       ovaries
in an unspoken play on the stereotype of Black men as a sexual threat to
white women. At first, we don't know that Simon is a Cylon. We see that
he is benevolent while helping Starbuck, blonde white and vulnerable,
recover from her injuries on Caprica. We want to believe (and not
entertain this historical thought because this is a progressive show) that
Simon (one of only two black men cast in the entire series) will not take
advantage of Starbuck. But then Starbuck awakes to find that she has
had surgery on her reproductive organs. While she was asleep, Simon
went inside her to sterilize her. And perhaps we are forced to see this in
one of two ways: 1) Simon as BLACK MAN HUMAN violates her, or 2)
Simon as BLACK MAN CYLON violates her. Once we find out he really
is a Cylon pretending to be human, then it's Simon represented as Black
man non-human who violates Starbuck reduced to her white female
reproductive organs. But that is only part of the story—the Cylons don't
want Starbuck to reproduce as it is hinted that she is somehow a special
threat. The Cylons have their own political agenda here, they mean simply
to survive, although some are inspired by love and revenge, and Starbuck,
fulfilling her mythic journey as it unfolds, turns out to be an angel of
death. But is this supposed to be a resurrection of the stereotype of Black
men, or its unconscious reiteration?

Alessandro Juliani (Chinese Italian Canadian) and Alexandra Thomas (ethnicity unknown). Alessandro Juliani plays Lt. Gaeta, looks racially mixed, for lack of a better description, and starts out being talented at following Admiral Adama's orders, quite efficient as Senior Officer of the Watch on the main deck, but after many episodes following orders explicitly, he becomes a political extremist who cannot tolerate a human/Cylon coalition and he helps stage a coup against the Galactica, for which he is shot by firing squad. Can a multiracial person be trusted? That's the racial stereotype that I dare say is suggested by the casting here—the mixed-race person as quixotic, unfathomable, unreadable, perhaps years of white actors playing yellowface as Charlie Chan and Ming the Merciless, etc., in which they appeared grotesquely neither, have conditioned American viewers to view Asians (in this artificial way) as abject. Yet the ideal of the mixed-race person is that she can identify with multiple races, like Obama has done politically, and therefore she is at the other extreme as a savior, one who can repair racial divisions, move humanity forward. We have Hera—child of Cylon Korean Canadian Sharon and of white human Helo. With her, the casting and story culminate in a kind of model minority rehash—Hera who is both human and Cylon—Asian and white—runs across a pristine field on the African continent on Earth, the perfect embodiment of our differences rolled into one utopia. And this has been argued academically—see Kent Ono who presents the mixed-race child—in *Come See the Paradise*—as a blank slate who takes on all of our qualities, an evolutionary gift, toward healing, toward peace, toward the leaving behind of our less-than-ideal monoracial past, as if forgetting were to be desired.

do you want to be that

Identity

The head came off

The breasts

The cock

The extra eye

The abdominal

The kneecap

The three toes

The cheek

The splendor

The buttocks

The elbow hinge

The thumb

The nose ring

The lower lip

The upper lip

The left wing

The suprasternal notch

The crossbow

The asshole

The tongue

The zipper

The morning

The afternoon

The dark strain

The cowboy

The craft

The eavesdropper

The Pelosi Bill

The sharecropper

The horizon

The Datsun 510

The pursuit

The Michael Jackson

The blue cross

The mailman

The double deluxe

The banana shake

The crossover

The metal years

The dead jello fish

The tight fitting jeans

The crease

The Mormons

The Fugiamora

The Great America

The torrential rains

The raisinette

The crimes against humanity

The Regal Beagle

The Boss Hogg

The Blair, Julie, and Kim

The doggie

The cat

The turkey mix

The Don Ho

The anathema

The spotted tree

The morse code

The moonrise

The moonset

The dog pee

The horse shit

The new sprinkler system

The haloed candy corn

The fresh Muzak

The coroner said

The prize

The cow

The American fly

The shattered window

The nuisance

The farewell

The frog with orange hair

The large cry

The Simpsons

The Atari

The other world

The constant clicking of tongues

The marching band

The ruby satellite

The Darth Vader twice for Halloween

The brown teddy bear

The fragrant girl

The field of grass

The coroner's request

The game

The snooze button

The near midnight

The overall goal

The offset

The eye opener

The recapitulation

The body is not human

The unbroken circle

The San Jose, California

soft memory
at 8 a.m.

History, Sawato

tired of talking about the beatings, how my grandfather **Sawato beat** his sons, my mom said she once saw their father kick her brother George across **the room** and George would get up smiling which would enrage Sawato even more ending with **more fists** and slaps across the head and face and pushing to the ground again. I can't believe that the beatings were done **only because** Sawato had been beaten himself, of course there was the incarceration of **my family** in Poston, Arizona during WWII—but there may have been more reasons, a hard life as **a sharecropper** before and after the war, his entire family that grew to 5 sons and 6 daughters in the **Santa Clara** Valley picking strawberries, and more research might reveal other conditions **that circumscribed** their world— white-owned farms, 1950s television and Hollywood films **that shaped** the public and private gaze of us by others. My rolling up of my sleeves is genetic? Perhaps **my grandfather** Sawato in the strawberry fields with his family and sometimes **other farmworkers** that he hired in order to stay somewhat cool rolled up his sleeves? Why did I have to come from **the fields** instead of the middle-to-upper-class white society that I saw on television? His face, as if saying I **am sorry** to me, on his technological deathbed at O'Connor Hospital. Oxygen tubes in his nose and his look of going **to die** and not being able to tell me what I needed to know, from this **grey-shirted** patriarch who used a soap that smelled strongly of talcum? Sawato who spoke **only Japanese** but could read the newspaper in that language once showed me how **to boil** a crab. Or rather, I stood beside him during a family gathering when he took that store-bought crab out of **some kind of** container and it was still alive and I marveled how it moved like a giant **shell spider** as Sawato dropped it in a large pot to boil. I did not know Japanese and he did not **know English,** so we both laughed. I wrote a long poem once about Sawato and me **sitting outside** on some imaginary porch and we are drinking beers watching the sun set. And somehow we **communicate to** each other in a familiar way, perhaps like we did briefly and wordlessly with the boiling crab in real life, and after **this imagined** communion, we decide it's time to go **back inside** the house which I began to describe in detail in terms of our activities there but quit before going too far in **the poem**. My grandfather died in 1988 at the age of 79, had dementia, fell down. Did he ever sing? **He laughed** again when he saw me playing cards with my uncles in their sharecropper's shack on the **strawberry field**. My mom warned me not to show him my money. Sawato used to spray insecticide throughout **the house** during the summers from a red-hosed canister pointing it everywhere that he possibly could

Shame

you have given up

on your self in

some way, that mirror

which reflects your face

against your perception of

a normal face—vibrant,

healthy, oceanic—is not

yours, but theirs, in

your belief that the

imagined world creates it

From Sam

my mother listened at the kitchen table while Sam
her brother-in-law spoke about his back pain due to the
removal of two vertebrae which reduced his height by
three inches and almost no medication helped and he
wanted to shoot himself he said until he purchased
cannabis cream from a San Jose dispensary he can walk now but his
face looked sallow that Christmas Day in his Gilroy
home where my mother's side of the family gathered
I was glad Sam found some relief and
somehow we segued into talking about the
camps he said he was six years old when he went to
camp he remembered it was hot and he had to walk far
to the latrine or restroom and there was sand everywhere
in their barrack in their food in the mess hall he remembered
crunching his teeth on sand
and he repeated again and again how hot it was in the
Arizona desert at Poston where his father met my mother's
father on trips outside of camp to work in
agricultural fields during the day for the government for little pay
years later my mom's sister Chiyeko and Sam would
get married and Sam remembered how virulent
the racism was immediately after the war in Gilroy recalling
how a white man called Sam's father a dirty Jap in a
dry goods store and told the father in front of the son to
get the fuck out and Sam stopped going to that store
with his father which had to be humiliating
I asked if his parents
ever spoke about the camps they didn't and I asked
if he knew how they felt about going to camp and Sam's
eyes widened he said how do you think they felt how
would you feel if your entire family had to go there a prison and I
didn't feel it at first although I could certainly acknowledge
his pain intellectually until a few days later when I retold
the story to someone else and I began to cry I later imagined Sam
and Chiyeko and their kids my cousins who I've known all
my life forced to get on a train to go to the desert because
that's how it would have been for someone my age my generation

to be rounded up and put in concentration
camps today as Trump would suggest it with his
willfully ignorant followers
all of us punished for being
illegal due to gender skin color sexual orientation and class careful
not to persecute those who are poor and white and male today a Black
man yelling
at Berkeley police is forced into a
squad van and off to jail while a homeless white man is given all
the time and patience to rant and yell and move freely within a circle
of the same white officers
we saw this from the coffee shop
my coworkers who were brown and white and me
we wanted to take our cellphones and record
the Black man being arrested
because those white men could not tolerate him
a threat to their white masculine authority which
operated vehemently in the 1950s when Sam was a young man
in Gilroy working on the farm a sharecropper like my
grandfather and my mother picking strawberries all
day in the sun
my mother would later turn to books and movies
as a result of her father who purchased the newspaper in Japanese
who took her and her siblings to watch Japanese films in
San Jose and elsewhere along that circuit

a sea or field of

as my mom quietly listened to Sam and me
talking at the table Sam's experience attracted other
listeners such
as my aunt Nancy in the front room and Sam's daughter Barbara who
walked past
several times and I wondered if Sam meant to emphasize near Barbara how
hard he worked in those early days
raised a family with two jobs bought a house with barely enough money
he said his children never believed how hard things were

Sam is 80 now and while talking for two hours about his life
the color returned to his face
he did not want to be filmed or recorded
after all these years
he did not want to say anything wrong

Dear, or Un-Dear, Man in the Compact Sedan, Who Said, "You're about to Learn That the Hard Way"

I was just a side-show casualty
to your ready rage
as you navigated
that narrow North Berkeley street,
screaming at the cars in front of you
to move as they stopped
to let another car back
out of a driveway. You bellowed
like some young men I've known
from my old neighborhood
in San Jose
on the Northside—
men beaten down as boys
and hardened into a curved
back and all anger,
ready to be triggered.
You hurled your self
at those stopped cars
as I walked past
on my way home.
I was tired
from the long day.
I purchased
some groceries that I carried
in my right hand,
stepping methodically
almost like in a trance. And you were there,
in your compact sedan,
screaming on the quietest street
you could drive down
to pass through
this white,
sleepy neighborhood.

Where were you going?
Back to anywhere?

As the cars in front of you moved again,
you started to inch forward. Why
did I make eye contact
knowing it would only incite
your rage again? What was I looking for
when you yelled back at me,
"Go back to China, old man!" When you added,
"You're not wanted here!" And
when you finished with,
"You're about to the learn that
the hard way!"

You drove so slowly
as if you might stop
and show me
the hard way
that you promised.
And I wondered

—who are we?

My Mother Might Be a Steller's Jay

While washing the dishes
I suddenly recall that my mother
is gone. She will not be there
to hear my complaints.
Or smile or laugh at my sarcasm.
She is a phantom person like a phantom
limb of memory. My feeling for
the world at times relies on her
being there. Now she is gone. And
I try not to go further into that space.
Perhaps I believe she is now a
Steller's jay in the neighborhood. Because
I called out my abandonment
and a Steller's jay replied, perched
on a phone line outside my window.
It's black head and blue body the colors
my mom would have liked. And it's rough caw or rasp.
Later in the day, I saw it again perched
on a roof. I tried
to take a picture of it and it flew
away. Typical, my mom never liked
taking photos. She rarely looked at
the camera. I always thought it
was my fault. Perhaps something
about not wanting to be captured
by the too often male gaze, even
her son's. Or was it a
reflex by the time I was born?
To be there and not look at
anything, or appear not to look.
Weeks later I saw two Steller's jays
on another roof playing together or perhaps
conversing with great animation, as
one flitted about leaving the other one
alone for a moment.
My mom liked to
be alone. She did not want

to be bothered.
So few people ever knew
her, as if she came and went
without much notice.
In her illness, her memory loss became my
memory loss. Did she
remember taking me to see that
popular movie when I was five;
if she can't remember, then do I remember,
and did we ever see it together?
That memory lodges
in the body and depends on
her body being present that
now gone, the result
is that perhaps no memory exists; we never
saw that movie together. I have
now seen it alone.
When two people
make a memory together, and one of them
dies, the memory becomes hollow, or hard to locate.
It cannot be conjured as before
because the connection to the other
that made it, is gone.
Still, this explanation does not satisfy. So
let me stop and say my mom
is a Steller's jay, a bird native
to the western third of North America. I
might hear one now in the distance as
I write this. That unmistakable, double caw or rasp.
I have probably been listening to it
forever.

New Relations

Eleanor's Pete kept in touch
after his death
via hummingbirds
and haranguing others
to tell her he's fine

*

dinner with Bachan & Eleanor
was nice despite
the salty fish
Bachan wishes she
had met me earlier
and spent more time with me
Eleanor, like Anita's mother, said
I am a "treasure" to Bachan
tonight we sat at Yu-Zen
with the cold wind
blowing the blue cloth
in front of the door

*

Hideko said I have a "big pain"
in my left shoulder—she did some
energy work on me there—
once she knows where
the problems are she can help me
remotely—
she gave me a small
atom-shaped crystal
to keep during the day—
Thanks, Hideko

*

Eleanor always wanted to write a novel
about Bachan's life—
she's a very strong woman and
she doesn't think she is,
said Eleanor

*

Bachan seems quite happy today

*

Sharon said she saw a psychic,
London Wildwind, who told her
that she had been married to a slave
in a past life and that she was a
lesbian who died a horrific death
but London would not tell her how

*

painful when looking back—

beauty of impeded speech

An Autobiographical Conversation

I think it was the war

that made him

the way he was.

Granny turned out

fine, but he never

got over it.

What did he do after the war?

Picked strawberries.

We moved to Morgan

Hill and worked on

a farm there. Then

moved to San Martin for a

while. No electricity.

I remember we had to

walk through a dark

door in order to take

a bath every night.

Who was born in the camps?

Tak was already born.

After him I came and

then Ken and Chiyeko.

Oh no, Chiyeko wasn't born yet.

Where'd they go?

To Poston.

What'd they do?

Well Granny stayed

home and watched

the kids while

Grandpa worked

I guess.

What kind of work did he do?

I don't know.

I don't think even

Granny knew.

He probably

did manual labor

or field work.

Granny said

he used to leave

in the morning

and come back

in the evening.

What did Granny sound

like when she talked about

the camps?

She wasn't sad.

She just talked

about it as if it

were nothing really.

As if it were a normal,

routine, everyday

part of her life?

Yes.

Grandpa never said
anything?

No.

Who was born after Chiyeko?

George, and then
June. Laura and
Nancy. Richard.
And Judy and Jackie.

Didn't they ever wonder
what it was like to be
in the camps?

Yes, but they didn't
ask all the time.

Did everyone pick strawberries

after camp?

Yes, except Granny.

Was it hot?

Of course it was!

Insects?

Yes.

Did you wear gloves?

No.

What's the most memorable
image you have of those
days?

It was just all of us
kids picking strawberries all day.

That's it? Nothing else?

That's it. That's

all we did really.

Besides go to school.

No great experiences?

No adventures?

Nothing really happened.

Nothing bad ever

happened until Grandpa

and George died.

How come no one except

Granny cried at their

funerals?

I know.

I guess everyone was glad

to get rid of Grandpa,

and, since George was all

alone, he had no one

to cry for him—

except Granny.

I think I'll learn

Japanese and talk

to Granny about

her stay in the camps.

What?

I think I'll learn

Japanese and talk

to Granny about

her stay in the camps.

Oh. Why don't you.

Then I'll show her

that video about the camps.

Oh. Why don't you.

Steve Fujimura is a poet based in Berkeley, California. His writing engages with memory, history, loss, and family. His work can be found in *New American Writing, Milvia Street Art & Literary Journal, Essential Truths: The Bay Area in Color*, and other publications. He has participated in programs with The Community of Writers in CA, the Berkeley Poetry Festival, the Hweilan International Artist Workshop in Taiwan, and Kearny Street Workshop's APAture festival. Steve earned an MA in creative writing at San Francisco State University. He is from San José, CA.

www.ingramcontent.com/pod-product-compliance
Lightning Source LLC
Chambersburg PA
CBHW021205090426
42740CB00008B/1240